Material Matters
Clay

Terry Jennings

Chrysalis Children's Books

First published in the UK in 2003 by

(6) Chrysalis Children's Books

64 Brewery Road
London N7 9NT

© Chrysalis Books Plc 2003

Text by Terry Jennings

ISBN 1-84138-819-X

British Library Cataloguing in Publication Data
for this book is available from the British Library.

A Belitha Book

Editorial Manager: Joyce Bentley
Series Editor: Sarah Nunn
Design: Stonecastle Graphics Ltd
Picture Researcher: Paul Turner

Printed in China

10 9 8 7 6 5 4 3 2 1

Picture credits:
Corbis: page 10 © Roger De La Harpe; Gallo Images/Corbis.
Hanson: pages 22-23, 26.
Poole Pottery: pages 14-15, 16 (left), 19.
RMC Readymix: pages 24, 25 (top), 27.
Roddy Paine Photographic Studios: pages 1, 4, 5 (right), 6, 16 (right), 17, 25 (below), 28-29.
Spectrum Colour Library: page 18.
Stonecastle Graphics: page 5 (left).
Sylvia Cordaiy Photo Library: pages 9 (right), 11, 12-13, 21.
Terry Jennings: pages 7, 20.
Wheal Martyn, Cornwall: pages 8, 9 (left).

contents

Using clay

We use things made from **clay** every day. Most cups, saucers, plates and jugs are made of clay. Clay is also used in houses and other buildings

Some of the many objects made from clay.

Clay is a **natural material** that comes from the ground. Moist clay is soft and smooth. When clay is dried it goes hard. When clay is baked in an oven, it goes very hard and cannot be softened again.

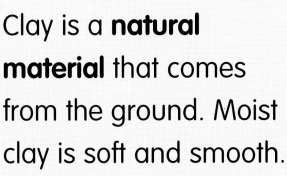

How clay is formed

Clay is made up of pieces of rock so tiny that they stick together.

Clay often contains the fossils of plants and animals that lived millions of years ago.

When it is wet, clay is soft and easy to shape.

Rivers and streams slowly wear away the rocks that they flow past.

The tiny pieces of rock in clay came from larger rocks. The large rocks were broken down by the weather and by rivers, streams and the sea. The bits of rock broke into smaller and smaller pieces. The smallest pieces became clay.

Where clay comes from

There are many different kinds of clay. All the clay we use is dug out of the ground from large **pits**. Some clay is dug with spades. But now most of it is dug using large machines.

Digging clay with a spade is hard work.

The clay washed out of this huge pit will be used for making fine **pottery**.

When the paper for this book was being made, clay was added to it to make it smooth and shiny.

In some pits, the clay is washed out using water. Huge hoses fire water at the sides of the pit. The clay is later separated from the water.

9

Hand-made pottery

Moist clay can be made into many shapes by bending, twisting or squashing it. The first pots were made by hand. Clay was rolled into long, thin pieces, like worms. These long rolls of clay were then coiled round a flat circle of clay.

This pot is being made from coils of soft clay.

This ancient Greek vase was made by hand more than 2,000 years ago.

About 9,000 years ago, people in Turkey and Iran learned that baked clay pots do not soften in water.

Pots were also made by pinching the clay until it became the right shape. The first pots were dried in the sun. Later, people learned how to bake the clay pots in special ovens, called **kilns**.

shaping clay

Today, the quickest way to make round pots by hand is to use a **potter's wheel**. The **potter** puts a ball of wet clay in the middle of the wheel.

The potter shapes the clay with her fingers as it turns round on the wheel.

This potter is smoothing the top of a pot.

These clay objects have been baked and decorated.

When the pot is the right shape, the potter leaves it to dry. Later the pot is baked in a kiln.

Fine, thin pottery that you can see light through is called china or porcelain. It was first made in the country of China.

Firing and glazing pottery

On its own, baked clay looks dull. It is also **porous**. This means that it lets water through.

The pots on these shelves have been stacked ready for baking, or firing as it is called, in the kiln.

To make pottery look better, it is covered with a **glaze**. A glaze is a thin layer of liquid glass. The glass makes the pottery look shiny. It also **waterproofs** it.

This is the glazing room of a pottery.

This vase has been coated with glazes of several different colours.

Decorations

You need a steady hand to decorate a pot.

Pottery is often **decorated**. The easiest way to decorate pottery is to make a pattern of marks in the clay while it is still soft.

This pot was decorated with a different coloured clay before it was baked and glazed.

16

Some expensive pottery is painted by hand. Other pottery is painted by machine or has **transfers** stuck on it. A few kinds of pottery are decorated with different coloured clays.

This plate was decorated with a transfer before it was glazed.

Moulding clay

Most cups and mugs are made in a factory. Water is mixed with the clay until it is runny like cream.

This man is checking cups and mugs as they come from a kiln.

A machine pours the clay into a **mould**, which is shaped like a cup or mug. When the clay in the mould has dried, it **shrinks** slightly. The mould is then opened and the cup or mug is taken out. The handle is put on before the cup or mug is baked and glazed.

This teapot, cup and saucer were made in a mould.

Building with clay

Clay is used as a building material. In some hot, dry countries, such as Mexico, clay bricks are shaped and then dried in the sun. The bricks are stuck together with very wet clay to make walls.

These houses in Britain have walls made of clay mixed with sand, gravel and straw.

Drying clay bricks in the sun in Mexico.

In countries where there is a lot of rain, bricks, roof **tiles** and clay water pipes have to be baked in a kiln to make them waterproof before they can be used.

Brick-making today

Making bricks by machine.

Most bricks are made by machine. Clay is dug from the ground by huge machines. It is then broken up and moistened. The wet clay is forced through an opening so that it forms a long, narrow ribbon. It is a bit like toothpaste being squeezed from a tube.

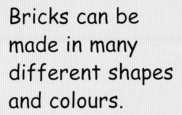

Bricks can be made in many different shapes and colours.

Wires cut the ribbon into bricks. The bricks then pass through a long kiln, which bakes them.

The world's largest brickworks is in Bedfordshire, England. It can make more than 10 million bricks in a week.

Cement and mortar

Cement is an important building material. It is made by mixing dry clay with crushed limestone rock. When the mixture is heated, it turns into the grey powder, cement.

Dry clay and crushed limestone rock are heated in this tall building to make cement.

24

Cement being poured from a mixing machine at a building site.

When cement is mixed with sand and water, it makes a paste called **mortar**. Mortar is used to stick bricks or concrete blocks together.

A man in Essex, England set a world record building a wall with mortar and 747 bricks in 60 minutes!

A bricklayer using mortar to stick bricks together in a wall.

concrete

A special mixer lorry is used to take wet concrete to a building site.

Concrete is another important building material. It is made by mixing cement, sand, stones and water together. Concrete doesn't have to be baked to harden it. It dries hard like rock on its own.

26

Some large boats with hulls made from thin concrete are able to float.

Large buildings are usually made of concrete that has steel rods in it to make it stronger.

These concrete blocks make a solid base for a new building.

Because it has steel rods in it, this concrete bridge will be very strong.

Do it yourself

Clay in soil

Most soils contain some clay. How much clay does the soil near you contain?

1 Wearing gloves, put a handful of soil in a clear plastic jar with a lid.

Now try a different soil. Does it contain more or less clay?

2 Half fill the jar with water.

3 Screw the lid on the jar and give it a good shake to mix the soil thoroughly. Now leave the jar to stand until the next day.

4 The soil falls into separate layers. The top layer is clay.

Glossary

cement A grey powder used to make mortar and concrete.

clay Tiny pieces of rock that stick together.

concrete A man-made rock used in building.

decorate To make something look more beautiful or colourful.

glaze A shiny layer of glass put on the outside of pottery.

kiln An oven used for hardening or drying bricks and pottery.

material A substance that is used for making something else.

mortar A mixture of sand, cement and water used to stick bricks together.

mould A container for making things set in the shape that is wanted.

natural Made or carried out by nature, not by people and machines.

pit A deep hole or hollow.

porous Something that allows water or air through it is said to be porous.

> **potter** Someone who makes pottery.

> > **potter's wheel** A special wheel used by a potter to shape pots and vases.

> > **pottery** Pots, cups, plates and other things made of baked clay.

shrink To become smaller.

tile A thin piece of baked clay used to cover walls, roofs and floors.

transfer A piece of paper with a picture or pattern on it that can be made to stick to a surface by soaking or heating it.

waterproof Something that keeps water out is said to be waterproof.

Index